## Also by Horace I. Goddard

*Rastaman: Poems for Leonta*
*The Long Drums*
*The Awakening and Song of the Antilles*
*The Journey Home*
*A Common Tongue: Interviews with John Agard, Cecil
    Abrahams, John Hearne, Wole Soyinka*
Phoebus and the Crow *(Children's story)*
*A Dog Named Sputnik* (Children's story)
*Paradise Revisited* (novel)
*Child of the jaguar spirit* ( novel)

# One People:
# Two Worlds Apart

HORACE I. (MUKWANO) GODDARD

**BALBOA.**
PRESS
A DIVISION OF HAY HOUSE

Balboa Press books may be ordered through booksellers or by contacting:

Balboa Press
A Division of Hay House
1663 Liberty Drive
Bloomington, IN 47403
www.balboapress.com
1 (877) 407-4847

Because of the dynamic nature of the Internet, any web addresses or links contained in this book may have changed since publication and may no longer be valid. The views expressed in this work are solely those of the author and do not necessarily reflect the views of the publisher, and the publisher hereby disclaims any responsibility for them.

The author of this book does not dispense medical advice or prescribe the use of any technique as a form of treatment for physical, emotional, or medical problems without the advice of a physician, either directly or indirectly. The intent of the author is only to offer information of a general nature to help you in your quest for emotional and spiritual well-being. In the event you use any of the information in this book for yourself, which is your constitutional right, the author and the publisher assume no responsibility for your actions.

Any people depicted in stock imagery provided by Thinkstock are models, and such images are being used for illustrative purposes only.
Certain stock imagery © Thinkstock.

Printed in the United States of America.

ISBN: 978-1-4525-9226-8 (sc)
ISBN: 978-1-4525-9227-5 (e)

Balboa Press rev. date: 3/21/2014

For
My sister Iona Odessa Browne
The Tamale and SSentongo families
Westmount Jamaican possée

# ACKNOWLEDGEMENT

This collection would not have come to fruition were it not for the gracious support of the Tamale family who allowed my wife and me to accompany them to Uganda in 2011. Their extended family greeted us warmly and accepted us into their clan with new names. I would also like to thank Derrilyn Morrison, associate professor of English, Macon College, who graciously edited the manuscript and made many timely suggestions. To my many Jamaican friends at Westmount Seventh day Adventist Church, walk tall.

# Contents

# Song of Uganda

This country of Uganda is steeped in the traditions
of the Baganda and here teeming tons
of black masses wear different masks

some of riches, some of poverty and others of high
or low land/ living. Children drink at the fountains
of death, defying serums that give life life

City slums dwell beneath towering high-rises,
towns of the rich, eye sores to the poor. This brown
mud spawns a variety of people

I see skin in asphalt black burdening day and
Roaming night. Nilotic noses curl towards
curbs of Bantu brown

This rich Uganda soil seeks an African owner
to restore its once kingly pride of people
The leaders are in hiding in this election tide

of mindless rivalry. The country is on edge and
tourists are turned away from Mandela Stadium, a
stage to national pride

Politicians promise, and then pronounce utterances
of disdain upon the railing crowds. The people
crowd the air with calls for a revolution for food,

for medicine, for roads that lack potholes burial
grounds for unsuspecting motorists Everywhere,
guns are pointed to silence opposing voices

# Makerere

Here the roll calls the learned
To degrees of mountain excellence
Makerere waves Oxonian flags
And slides forward with precision

The Who's Who of East Africa
Trod its sprawling grounds
Rats bit bite-sizes from all academic
Disciplines and left broken hearts behind

The storks strut about this hill
And heavy the air with
Unrepenting scents of their smell
Only the nose can discern the distinction

Students roam the grounds under
The marauding eyes of watchful guards
Here there are no strangers, except tourists
With their cameras and beguiling looks

A quick trot to the guard tower
Along buttressed walls of conversation,
Signals an all-clear to mingle with
The majestic birds honking from their perch

## African woman

I am African woman
See me go on bended knee
To provide my husband
With his dignity

I am African woman
Chiseled in the image of
my mother. Here I see the
Changing customs of a new generation

I am African woman
steeped in Western tradition
I am freely trapped
in centuries of custom

I am African woman
I do not reach three score
and two, for I breed
to feed extra mouths

I am African woman
gum-tied to this soil
My body supports my spirit
Spirited away, I survive

in a dark place. I roam
This land with its imperfections
It is still my shelter, my queendom
I am African woman, where shall I roam

# Houseboy

My name is Peter
I guard the gate
to this imperious mountain motel

I let clients in amidst the din
of midnight noises
My rest comes in the

Noises of the crickets
That lull me into wakeful
Sleep, yet I rise

When the horn sounds
Or when the driver calls
My sacred name I open

The gates of this serene haven
They call me Peter with the keys
keying the notes in and the music out

I wheel the iron gate in
and out, out and in
to let these denizens within

enjoy their priceless intent
of driving their motta car
in and out, out and in unceasing

I am Peter of the gate
I multi-task while I wait
For the next vagrant call

I sweep the grounds
grounds sweating my feet
I trim the hedges

Make pledges to a Canadian
Doctoring to the health of foreign
Women trying to dance like an African

In this New Year morning
In minus fifteen weather
Whether I wake or sleep

Run errands, protect
The prostitute from murder
It doesn't matter

This is my only job
Though Job could do no better
I like it here. It is my home

# Muzungu

My name is not Muzungu
Look at me carefully
My skin is sun-dried black

My eyes are Ugandan brown
My palms are varnished with
the red clay lying around

My head is flickering sunshine,
producing the heat of revolution
My sinews are filled

with River Nile beer
Listen to me and hear
My name is not Muzungu

# A Writing Attack

The muse is about
There is no doubt
that this mist

of a cool morning
is dawning new lines
That blacken this page

There is no rush
to close leaden eyes
that pry into distant stars

The melodies of the spheres
are captured on Antelope road
while sleep comes like a toad

hopping from an animal cover
on a bed snoring symphonies
And I write these steel lines

bursting forth from a brain
that ceases to shut down,
sprinting, routing words

on this page in a
mud flow of word rage until
the brain explodes in rain

## Ring of Antelopes

Kampala leaps
Kampala bounds
to the sounds

across her seven hills.
The music vibrates
and she gyrates,

lowering her body to the ground.
Catcalls herald the New Year
Men and women bend the air

with shouts of acrid glee
Smoke dances from burning tires,
fueling the pre-dawn merriment

Kampala halts
Kampala waltzes
around the clock

Soldiers at the ready
With AK 47's steady,
watch the raucous revelry

The citizens negotiate
by blockading the royal gate
and commanding them to articulate
peace to the New Year

# Mamie (Report to a Dead Mother)

Mamie, though you dead
and cahn understan'
I telling you wha happenin'

to me in this present life
of despair, heat crushing these
few grey hairs on me head

I am here in Uganda
whichin, it is in East Africa
I know we come from de West

But Mamie, all is de same
De people dem like we,
black like coal pot, unbleached

The only thing clear is them teet
Even de brown of them eyes turn
black, turn back from

coughing fire alive
It hot like Barbados,
but there is hardly any breeze

The people breeze along the street,
not minding to see if they
knock yuh over fuh get kill

Mamie, you won't believe
there is all kind o' police;
some wid black nuniforms;

some in white; some in
khaki and others in blue
dungaree, all carrying big gun

The country is a democracy
with a high police presence.
This show of force and power

force people fuh mind them business
and not busy body bout de guv'ment
seat of incorruption, giving

big jobs to supporters, and
choking off the opposition
The fires burning

all over the place
in this 2011 race
for president of this pearl

of Africa, wealthy with people,
fruits and ground food
Industrial pollution is

the price paid for modernization
And de pot holes in de road is
ruination to the rotation of wheels

You have flush pit
if you please that tease
you into squatting

Squatters have rights too,
even when they mess on you,
and Mamie there's a lot of that

The traffic doan follow
any particular direction
They cut you off,

going right or left
and these boda boda guys
flies with motor bikes,

rush like runnels of death,
four people sitting on this ride
swerving and curving to kill

your spirit, and motorists push
pass like them mad, shoving you
into the maddening crowd

only Thomas Hardy could
talk about so beautiful
a description and prosery

Beside that, I doing all right so far
The people, them real nice

I sitting here in the shade of
A Kampala restaurant that have a menu
men hardly able to eat for lack

of food in the place. So rice
and red sauce, brown in its ways,
colour the whiteness on the plate

with French fries on de side,
is a meal that hunger craves
and this real Bantu man

charcoal black, darkening
the day, sucks the chicken bones
and snap at the white basmati

rice, gulping with his gullet
like the pullet he guzzling.
Now the evening getting fresh

My wife is on Antelope hill
Wishing she was still
With me instead of

heating up the air wid
worry. I only went to get clothes,
not wind blows of worry

This is Uganda in its pride,
in its stride for African fame
and the people playing no game

# Kiyera (Nile) River

Old Nile lurks on her perch
High in the Jinja mountain forest

Then in the dark of night
She flaps her wings violently

Oil leaks from her sprawling
Feathers, winging her to the north

Falls fall from a broken beak
building water swings that Owen claims

The government submerged
the forks of this sensuous intercourse

to power the lamp lights of
Jinja and her sub counties

Tourists come and take delight
in the tranquility of Uganda

Blue, searching for the spot
spotting from river craft

the real source of Egypt's
Cleopatra's whiteness

Blue on blue from sea green
pelting her way north,

riding Poseidon's tropic waves,
searching for bounty in

Nubic Sudan, painting
Mud castles for Kings,

long since covered with silt
Now the rhythm changes

and the churlish lips
spout spumes of long horn

cows, milk too rich to
support the blackness of

this ancient land
Musa sailed along her Egyptian banks

In his reed cradle, Musa
waited to hear from the

king's craving daughter,
who fussed over hymn/him

to Pharaohnic Africa,
north of here where I stand

Cleopatra missed this playground
Her royal youth, compass free,

could not navigate the crowning
hordes of fierce warriors

their spears at the ready
to pierce her royal rawhide

So Hollywood framed the
Queen in a sheen of white

The world absorbed the dye
And a new queendom was born

Nile crests, Nile bursts,
flooding the river banks

with corn, fields of barley,
wheat, millet and sorghum

beat out rice fields
on the threshing floor

And so I came, saw
The blue truth of

breaking waters travelling
through a garden of her story

More than six millennia ago,
Musa wrote his scripts

and henceforth we follow his guide
and ride the pages of worship

to Yahweh who brought us
Yeshua, savior and king

triumphant over sin and death
Ugandan jiggers worm

their way through worn out flesh,
pulsing into death of a nation

Conquered by child soldiers
And the army sounds an alert

to prevent terrorists acts
as the boda boda riders

plunge the country into mourning
Old Nile dances her cha cha cha

through perilous times,
revealing her unyielding strength

of diameter, of power
to deliver Egypt from sectarian terror

Mists rise.
      Mists spread
Wings        wings        flapping
White protective feathers
      Reassuring the land
          of creation day

Mists guide
      Mists ride
over    and    over/lapping themselves
Hills and valleys hover
      to cover the day with coolness,
          to dry the footsteps beneath our feet

# Uganda's Rain Dance

The rain dances with heavy feet
on these Ugandan busy streets

The water makes a play
for anything blocking its way

Yesterday's fields of potatoes
become today's yams.

There is no recompense from nature
and farmers are left to sort out the matter

Some argue for more than their share
of the new crops, and build animosity

in this great country, subsisting
on food planted to feed their family

Some wetlands receive goods
by stampeding flows of water

The marshes welcome the downpour
to keep alive the ancient plants

of papyrus to scribble the
death toll on for future forget

Bodies pile up in the muddy
streams and screams echo

across the shifting hillsides
burdened with mountain boulders

The government hollers its best
while the opposition cries for rest

from tyranny and one man's
necromancy. They arrested the

witch doctor bewitching
those who dare come closer

After twenty five years
the nation lays its arms

arms to wrestle for
education, health care

and the fight goes on
shifting the focus on the

Father President, who prays
at his residence for divine

Providence to keep him in power
to better the lives of his people

# Negotiating Traffic in Kampala

Tremors of noise explode on the roads
The aftershock scatters crowds of vehicles
along the choking Kampala roads
Two-lane traffic trap drivers
and walkers in pedestrian suicide

Diesel deadens the lungs
with choking satisfaction
and bloats bodies with polluted air
Death chases life trying to find its source
as it forms a quick end to a short beginning
The Blue Nile of ancient lore

What is life when thirty five
million in vehicular strife
struggle to gain a shilling
crafted in the image of mourning

The Boda Boda brags of roadside death
with mother, child and a stranger strapped
to the back of this taxi motorcycle

Cycle of birth and death
hurry between moving vehicles
and along crowded sidewalks as these
taxis hurry to make a dollar

Death perches behind the wheel,
replacing kneecaps and
Steel- rimmed limbs, and pushing madness
beyond the brink of normalcy

This is Uganda, the land of plenty
which gives much to the wealthy
The poor is with us always
So kill the chickens and live today

## Lake of Fire

The sky bleeds fire
over the Ethiopian coast
KLM 0593 bobs and weaves
negotiating its high pathway
through mountainous air space

The daunting layers of black
Beat back clouds about to sleep
The sun streaks slowly to its rest
The poet sits back and reminisces
about Uganda's burdening yoke

Remnants remain of its oppression
kraaled in small shops
They never sought their birthright here,
but maintained British passports and a fare
ready to run with the country's wealth

Today hidden in small spots
Crunched down behind Blacks
They quietly fear Idi Amin's ghost.
One more fear fills the air
And flings caution to the wind

At forty-one thousand feet
speeding along at eight hundred
and fifty-five miles, a baby cries
Clouds of white mists mass the night

# The Washer Woman Stoops

The washer woman bends low
Below her shifting hands
with a purple rag, she moves over

the tiled floor adroitly
Not a speck is left behind
The mop pleads with her to

be used, but she moves on
from room to room until
all is spotless and clean

She wrestles with every corner,
back arched like a bow
Then she speeds into action once more

She's afraid to cover up
but there's no one around
To prevent her from her sound

Swooshing the cloth with motooke
strength,
Back arched, arching up
without broom in each room
until the tiles shine clean

# Washer Woman

The washer woman bends
Over the wash basin
Of mud caked clothes

She jucks and rubs
and pounds the stains
from T-shirts and pants alike

The mistress warns her
That nothing must rest on the ground
The grass covered earth is out

With care she toils until
out of breath, and then she pauses
She needs the four thousand shillings

When the job is quite done
she bends down and unrolls the clothes
then gently clips them to the line

The wind fights with the humidity
The clothes remain damp
To scttle the score, the sun

steps out of its door
and burns the clothes bone dry
The washer woman leaps for joy

Her wash is plucked from the heat
and is placed inside to cool
The mistress is pleased

She folds with care
All the clothes that were there
smelling of sundried goodness

# Black K (Night)

Darkness rides the night
embraced by hovering Black
Still is the silence from dusk
to dawning morn

Whispering silence whips
White thoughts that collide
crash and crush into lines
cascading into stanzas.

Stanzas dance in tune
with the silence, with
the blackness, with a
drawn out prayer for beckoning light

Safety is trudging between
layers of darkness that
lead to a cloistered bathroom
Safety is searching for light in darkness

The silence cuts the night
Banana trees and coffees leaves
kiss in the black mists
producing green bands of fruit

In this pearl of sprawling Africa
where thunder-hewn hills
and mist-formed valleys
hug, there is no fear of the dark

## Kiyuini Road

Clouds fight on the mountain sky
with flaming swords clashing
clanging and drizzling blood

The lumbering sky gods
shout across the cavernous valleys
The children refuse to stop the fight

Mortally wounded players
cry thickened blood
That drip drops upon the sodden land

Blood hits the brown earth
pulverizing her soft skin
and running in ever-widening slopes

The soft road becomes gooey
Flesh descends damaged/filled eyes
Deep veins are cut and flow

Passage becomes impassable
as passengers dismount
to free the Galeria from doom

Fear mounts as thoughts
of drowning swell with every prayer
The truck is pressed in mud

The drag shaft is snapped
like a brittle twig
The driver cooks while he waits

Waiting in the mud, shouting
and waving motorists to stay clear
of a treacherous ditch ahead

Galeria picks its way through
Silent prayers of Adventist
Christians ascend on high

Quick is the response
God's promise is fulfilled
We are saved by His Grace

# Noise in the Compound

Midnight screams
Bounce around the starry night
The residents awake

to see if there is smoke
in the compound. Fire is there
as a Kenyan man demands

his pleasures from a night
worker. The occupants run out
as the woman takes flight

The caretaker is there
to prevent her murder
as the man pursues her, intent

on gaining his due share
of bittersweet pleasure
She is quickly pushed

into the caretaker's hut
where she yells in defiance
her unwillingness to provide
her flesh at any cost

# Uncle

Nameless one no eyes
to see what lies around you
You think that all is well
Wells of despair curl your
white hair and you sit and
wait for the gods to return

Your ears record your world,
the happenings and misgivings
You sit and imagine times past
The forest is no longer your playground
Your body now ground to a halt,
feebly gathers its weight

You stand at the door
glimmering, tracing the sounds
of your kin as they wave goodbye
Then you crawl back to your seat
the brief moment passing by

# Kiboga Child

Child of this Kiboga soil
your mud-baked skin coils
and wraps itself in banana leaves

Oil is the teardrops of mud
that bathes your black skin
Your body is Jackfruit

Pineapple and pawpaw
give fragrance to your breath
Avocado and mango flow

cholesterol free through your veins
In vain you struggle
to imprison yourself in tradition

Customs ignite a culture
Where women stoop before men
with knees rubbed down

carrying food to feed them
Ground food pressed on a plate
Crawling, bowing, cowering in obedience

## God be praised

I say Amina to my God in
Luganda as the ghost of

Amin Dada, hovers over the
Archbishop's death, by default

The body politic lives on
with life-reviving bullets

This killing of God's anointed
by a fearful power hungry

father while bowing to Allah
five times a day down on his knees;

heart and soft brain,
knees rubbed down under the weight
of bodies piled up in secret prisons

waiting to be eaten.The best parts
of liver are chewed and swallowed to
prevent a resurgence of evil

Milton who wrote of Paradise lost
regained his stature in the

matter of the people
versus a vicious dictator

He who created the Kabaka
President of this great Uganda,

now put him to flight to his
other kind/dom of Great Britain,

sanctuary for Africa's reposing kings.
His trusted general sends him

packing while he is abroad.
Eight years of purging, rid

the nation of sacred corruption
This is replaced by tribal ligation,

blotting out from birth the
life of leaders aspiring for power

Then Milton wrote Paradise Regained
and climbed the steps of the State House again

The bushes moved closer to Kampala
The antelopes' retreat

Then the opposition conquered the
hills and valleys with the rhetoric of war

Now the country has made progress
The President conducts state

prayers for heathen proselytes of
faith. This Christian man

demands loyalty to the Father,
stepping down politicians for Dada

Who dare oppose you, Father
of a fix-it-up nation

of restored kingdoms of
Busoga, Baganda and

others, keeping peace with
the nation, until later, much later

## Black Men in Motion

Everywhere I go men
in black, black men of the nations

have the same action
which I call satisfaction

from work. Cards flip
hurried fingers on tables

Dominoes ring hard surfaces
Vibrating divine music to

their gods. They roll the dice
trying to win rice for

empty stomachs at home
Sugar water and bakes

is all it takes
to debilitate the children

From generation to generation
men suck the breasts of inaction

Stone drunk, they hurry home
no shame on their foreheads

and demand a full share
of food paid for with services that day

The man child grows up not
knowing his real papa

The circle is never broken
at the seams of Black nations

## Explosion of Power

Jinja Hills flow north
with warnings of wrath

Sparring rivers and lakes
disturb the peace in the wake

of political turmoil
The Electoral Commission

Gun up with AK47s
Cameras are afraid to click

and flash in this place
of securing the next president

Stark faces preside over
streets walking beats of

righteous indignation
The people dem walk

gingerly eating ginger cookies
and drinking Stoney Ginger Ale

This is the pale of things to come
when the silent railroad

baron will come in glory
again to reign/rain over we

# Orphan Child

I am an orphaned child
I am destined to roam
in the wild of things here

Bear with me and give
me a hundred shillings
That is not too much to give

I am ragged and worn out
My stomach is empty
walking about these dusty roads

My parents died from want
of midnight pleasures
in the shadows of this barren hut

I am orphan, unschooled
and ruled by the emotion of hunger
Help me to surrender to food

I am your brother
bred from this fertile land
Wars I did withstand,

but hunger is now my enemy,
boring with painful bullets
of disease though this body of mine

## Mzee (Old Man)

The old man dressed in his tunic
Summons the clan to a reunion

Thoughtful elders ensconced on
Their bench thrones of power,

remind children and relatives
of their sacred duties to the tribe

Their eyes glitter hope of better
for the new Western-crafted litter

of children and new chiefs
proclaiming unity of purpose

of helping one another, of educating
those who follow. Love, peace

and prosperity ring in the ears
of these picanni steeped in

the warrior ways, in the glory days
when the Bakaka reigned supreme

Though the castles of shelter
are now thatched with mortar

the counsel is given in silent
laughter of pleasure: honour

your father and mother,
if you want to prosper

Love your daughter as your son
Protect and provide for them is the sum

of this clan that binds us in
a prison of ancient tradition

Stay free from idleness
in which spins yarns of distress

Hold fast to the love of God
within which is the tribe's salvation

Prayers are offered in Luganda
as the men seated on a hillock prepare

to eat their meals presented on bended
knees of wives and daughters

Then they slowly drift away
to far places in the silence of night

## Mr. President

Hills hang by their clay roots
cut out
by rain chisel
    drizzle
        drizzle
            by
    drops /full of water
        flow
    hammering lost strings
        of boulder/dash
        crash down
            roll down
        'pon iron head of clay
            break down
        unbrittle bone
        on marrowless stone
            thunder-claps of screams
        in the seams of the road
            running
            running
                cross land
        slipping and sliding
            into cement blocks
        of gated castles and
        water-patched roofs
        hallowing life inside
            dis/course of existence
and Victoria wakes in
        a British lake in de heart
        of we Afrika
that spawn Barak
        Obama white man
        saviour of

black whips of cotton licks
      dripping
      sugar juice
      in blood
      drops
      plop
      plop
spread across the land
in crimson bells
ringing, clanging
      down
      down
      with
      free-
      dom
      riders
on a donkey cart
loaded with plantation
dung
      down
at its roots of
present, past and future
survival of a nation
No condemnation
other than the Prez's obfuscation
of Africa
      sperm-seed
         of his extension
And bush: sersi, Lignum vitae,
HIV/aids tally up
      dat he did something
tangible, relateable to we
      pain
We own dear Prez
      we look to in four years

to wet/wipe
tears
of neglect
Reaffirm, confirm,
confound the cri*tics*
and do a little something
for the mother of the
earth people
here and there
Do something!
Lift hunger string!
Let children live
a little longer
here and there!
Share a little
Afrika son/sun

# Uganda Burning

Uganda burning
creating electricity from tires

Politicians argue about
New/found/land barrels

of black gold
Who will share

this precious commodity
of power and untapped

wealth of foreseen violence?
Jobs will be created

in the morticians vineyard
and the First Lady will glory

in fig leaf dresses, her
tresses braided with honey wax

and this western tribulation
of the need for more energy

will return the primal forests
to shade, food and shelter

Uganda burning to make food
in the city of his majesty

the Bakaka of Buganda
Air freshener of smoke

provokes unused airwaves
lung music sneeze in the breeze

of emphysema, producing
coal/era and black eyes

Uganda burning with hydro
electric dam/nuisance

only for the rich
lights of the poor

Tires provide holiday fun
as men monkey chatter
and baboon holler as they run

down
escarpments
     down mud
        hills of steps
     down stumped toe
       of agony
            for light
       for bright
       clouds
       for liberty

# The Ant Eaters

Wingtip to wingtip squadrons of white ants rise
Fluff the afternoon air and prepare to fight

Civilians crowd the space around the battlements
They outstretch dark hands and pluck the attackers

The ants are shielded in cavernous hangars
and are swallowed into protein obscurity

Belly rumbling noises disarm these bombers
Curiosity hastened the imagination into a series

Of questions: "What are you feeding on"
"Ants!" Came a terse reply, "very high in protein"

I sought shelter in the biblical dietary laws
Leviticus bound when I was asked to participate

I kept my religion and my lack of knowledge
Out of focus, for I was only an ignorant visitor
silently photographing the ecstatic scene

# Blood of Africa

Bowels of earth roar sulphurous black
Into a noonday sky spread-eagled
Across a crimson sun busy receiving
noises from freedom seekers

I hear presidential platitudes: "My
People love me. I will not step down,
Bow down to mortal men, mine enemies
I created this desert land into one of the best

I pump its oil to feed Western appetites
Now my children rebel against me
We are a finely crafted democracy
And you gave me all my powers

I will not step down, nor bend to terrorists
I will kill all instruders until my own blood
Ceases to flow in these desert veins deserted
by sounds of sons calling out for mothers

Your fathers are shot with hot bullets at the
Back of empty brains not able to discover fear
in their attackers' eyes, relieving them from shame
This desperate cry for freedom is a breach of loyalty

Regime change will not feed your children
I have eaten well and fed you likewise
When you yield your last breath, who will hear
you cry, desert crows, and answer the carrion call

Mother of terrorists in Washington Square
Who will chant to Allah but your mullahs
This young blood spilled on Africa's brackish sands
Will invite crows Caw! Caw! Call them when death

pervades the land and then they will run from the
worm-infested skins bloated and bubbling oil
In the house white on a cliff of indecision
Overlooking River Potomac, the gardener

plants roses for my head. There is a need for
vegetables to mix with the warriors' blood
The dogs of war hunger for true meat
to feed the children in their black infantry

Africa, behave and let me reign in peace'
Four years is all that is required for a lifetime of
perks: Secret Service for me and my family,
a presidential library to glorify my inactivity

I look forward to ending this term with pomp and
ceremony and wait patiently my crown of glory
The world will proclaim that nothing happened on
my watch, no wars other than those I inherited

No national disorders other than Wall Street
meltdowns cooled by trillion dollar coolants
Tsunamis were avoided in the midst of seismic
upheavals in Europe and down under

We prevented gore in the streets, Gore in the theatre
of global warming, gore in the stampedes of bulls
here and there. Jordan River is beckoning us to
come for a baptism of fire

At home we outfitted Canada's fleet to patrol Libya
and provided saline solutions to Qadaffi's fleet
holed up in port. Our babes walk St. Catherine
Street, pearly gates to mortal degradation of

seasonal values of vulvar pleasures, downgraded by
Sodom and Gomorrah. It is sweet to be
president at this time of tomorrow's Chinese
prosperity. This will be my legacy—indecision!

# Tribal Ligation

I have saved you from starvation my children
Has the opposition filled your water pots
I am your tree of life providing all your needs

I suffer with you, eat boiled potatoes and
Finger-pressed matooke in plantain leaves
Has peas and ground peanut sauce failed

to sustain your sodden appetites now
My children my children, where have you been
We went to the West to study, Tata

What have you learned there, may I ask
We have learned to fill the market places
and shout for our freedom from oppressors

Is that all that you have learned, tell me
We have learned that the cleaning rag breaks our
nails and makes us dependant on poverty

My children, my children, what are you carrying
in the folds of your skin? We are carrying
memories rolled in papyrus skins

We have also learned the white man's ways
We eat at tables with our husbands and children
We use knives and forks and cook on electric stoves

We will no longer spit at the fire between the bricks
We will no longer take our husbands' licks
We respect our traditions, but ask for change

Tata, our husbands now cook, mop the floor,
Diaper the babies and do much more
They even run errands for us each day

We, the wives, read books and watch television
We telephone our girl friends and make plans
For husband-paid vacations in foreign lands

Who teaches your sons and daughters the customs
of our people? We no longer study all the details,
for our traditions need a modern upgrade

We give a crash course before we arrive home
and tell the children to smile a lot to their
grand-parents. A few words of greetings will suffice

Do you feed them our ancestral foods: millet, rice
sorghum, barley and beans
No! No! No!

These are not born from African soil under
the shaded trees of the forest. They
are Westerners and prefer pasta pizza
and Chinese food, with fortune cookies

Will your sons return to seek a bride
There is no need, for women are usually
everywhere

Then what shall I do with the bulls that
I reared? Tata, weep not for lost times
Hold fast to dreams of a changing future

The drums will never cease, but the
dances will be new. Then dismiss me
my children. My eyes are growing

dim. There is no light in the darkness
and the future seems dim. Weep not for
me my children while doing your thing

# Victory

The President is still boss; the opposition has lost
Uganda's kingdoms are still intact

No fissures or fractures pull east from west
The Nile still flows north from south

The pineapple retains its sweetness
And we can eat them when we want

In the comfort of the people's Presidential jet
Jutting out from freed ports of democracy

Oil will soon flow and cover our land with
Blood of joy, of peace and wealth

The crown of victory remains mine
Mine is freedom in snake-pits of follies

Mine is liberty in chains of idle talk
Mine is wealth in the oil fields in the dark

Mine is the empty promises of campaign rhetoric
That soothes the souls of the unschooled

I know that we as a people are safe
guarded by loyal tribal chiefs in uniforms

I trust our ancient band of warriors who fought
from tree tops in Kampala and made freeways

to the people's presidential palace
My people sing of freedom marked by loyalty

Dance to the five kings upon their thrones,
installed through pledges of fealty to me

Tolerance is the snorting nozzles of AK 47's
Prosperity comes at a price paid to the under/taker

Instead, let us crave things from above
Heavenly treasures that bind this land Uganda

Put away tribal rites and rituals
Come and worship at martyrs square where
A story lies and is ready to be told

Let us not re-enact what already exists
Or cull new meaning from this acrid smell of death

Celebrate my continued reign in this territory
I am still here, lifted higher than before

My victory was foretold in the stars
That crowd our seamless black skies

Long live imperial Uganda
Long live ancient Nile

# Love Plea

On my knees I beg you
To love me please
As you fold me in your arms

I pledge to ignore your charms
Of infidelity for the sake
Of your millennium clan

Though I'm from another tribe
I surrender to you as my guide
Hoping for a better future

On my knees I promise
Honey, the sweetness of my suppleness
Be with me always, as I dance the high life

On my knees this dawn
Of a new year, remember
Do-do, I really love and care for you

When the darkness dampens
And the blackness subsides
I will be here, just waiting

When the music is down low
My heart thumps below
Its soft desires for your love

# Broken but not Defeated

I cannot live in my parents' house any longer
I am an unmarried girl with a family
I must build a home in the compound and stay there

I am not allowed to inherit my father's land for
Girls have no status in our traditions. But I can
Stay here as long as I wish, or until I die

If I die before I'm married, my children may stay
But not own any of the land, for I am a woman
My brothers cannot chase me from the land

I cannot bargain for any of my father's wealth
I know the traditions, for I'm a child of the clan
My name is registered as a child of this band

My brothers' sons will take the land
But here I defiantly stand, for I'm woman
I gave birth to these traditions a long time ago

I am now married to an older man
I am beautiful, have a light complexion,
And am highly educated for a villager

I studied at the university and then
Went abroad for higher learning
I met my husband in England

We went back home to get married
My relatives were very happy for me
Marriage was a step up in class

I will not cook my husband's meal today
The smoke causes me to cough and cry
When I stoop to blow the fire, it puffs at me

The three-legged pot hisses like a snake
When the yams begin to boil
I went away too long, living in England

Where my first son was born in London
I am now used to gaz and electric cookers
The pots are modern and cook without soot

I did not start the fire with my breath
My husband says the food is sweeter
When cooked in the three-legged pot

My husband travels widely around the world
But in Uganda he follows useless traditions
I warned him I will run away if he does not help

With the many chores and the children
He scolds me and tries to calm my fears
By telling me that we will soon return to the West

The coconut broom hurts my back
When I bend to sweep the yard
He must buy me a blower to clean

The leaves or get a gardener to tidy
this yard of mango fruits and coffee beans
It takes too long to clean and the baby cries

No I will not cook my husband's meal today
Even if he sends me back to my village
My family will not return the bride price

I gave him many sons who are more costly
Than fifty long-horn cows and bulls in the kraal
My husband likes to eat chicken but will not

Pluck the feathers or cut its scrawny throat
He chews the long bones and makes sucking
Noises as he guzzles the marrow down

After eating he leaves the plate on the ground
He can tell my in-laws that I am a bad woman
It matters little to me. I have his children

Who will comfort me when I get older
He should not fight me to cook food
Because my nails and clothes become dirty

My husband likes to eat matooke with bean
sauce. Yet he will not go to the market or
To the farm to fetch the heavy plantains

He shouts that cooking is woman's work
And that I should be glad to have a husband
He thinks that a woman's place

Is in the garden or in the fields tending
Sorghum, millet, corn and the coffee plants
I refuse to do such hard labour in the sun

When he insists that I go, I hide in the bushes
He has enough money to hire help, but refuses
For him, money grows on trees when the crops

Are plentiful and market day brings high returns
He keeps the money for himself and buys me
A hoe. My lappa is torn and I need a new one

It is fifteen years since we were married
I bore him five sons whom he loves
He insists that they stay at home

And go to school to be educated
He wants them to be professionals
I too have higher education from Western

Universities, but he feels that education
is wasted on women since girls do not
need it to work in the fields or raise

a family. This makes me sad
He likes to make cover me at nights
when the children are in bed

I will not let him touch me tonight
He tells me than he wants more sons
I am not a rabbit in the fields

I am an educated woman
Equal to any man
I will not yield my life

Here I stand, co-equal
Qualified and ready to lead
I am new metal in this land

Progress has given me rights
as a human. Change must come
if we are to build this nation

I respect our traditions
of leadership by men
and all I ask is for them

to understand that women
are no second class citizens
We breast-fed these nations

## Broken and Defeated: A Husband's Response

I am a Baganda man
Our traditions spans centuries
My wife is Bunyoro

She criticizes our African customs
Because she lived in the West
She is angry about the patriarchal system

She doesn't like going to the fields
Nor sweeping the compound
She complains that it is too much work

There is a division of labour among our people
The woman must prepare meals, clean
The compound and look after the children

A man cannot do those chores
The villagers will shun him
The man must work outside the home

Besides, a man must have many sons
To fight for the clan and renew its name
A woman should bear many sons

If she bears daughters they must help
Her work at home and in the fields
Daughters take wealth from the family

There is much value in sons
While daughters are costly to keep
We must give their husbands money

To take them off our hands
I try to tell my wife that in the West
I can help her but not in Africa

My friends would laugh at me
And my relatives would disown me
If I am caught doing woman's work

When my wife gets angry
She reminds me that she is educated
And that her values are different

She cannot cook with wood
And complains about the lack
Of electricity in the country

She likes things of luxury
But these appliances are
Not functional in a country

That lacks the basic necessities of
Living in rural areas. We gather
Water from streams and walk home

We use a pit for a toilet and bathe
In the open behind the bushes
My wife expects a better life

And fails to understand that it is
Not yet possible in this land
Sometime she refuses to cook my

Food and I want to beat her
In the West I cannot touch her
They are laws against family violence

Here we flog disobedient wives
and children since they belong to us
Westerners do not understand our customs

A wife is a man's possession. He pays
for her with cattle and goats. The
Bride price can be very expensive

Her family placed a lot of demands
on me. If she complains to them
They are liable to take her back home

I live under these constant threats
Sometimes my wife refuses me
Unless I meet her material wants:

New shoes, new lappas and pocket money
This makes me feel less than a man, for
A man controls his household

My wife knows that I need more sons
To carry on the clan's traditions
She argues she is liberated

And will do as she pleases
I cannot return her to her family
Because of my five sons

I love my wife dearly and try
To explain my position in the house
I make all the decisions

She obeys and carries them out
A disobedient wife brings grief
And strife to a man's family

A clan cannot be strong without unity
My wife thinks our ways are old-fashioned
She copies the lifestyle of the rich

The women sit at home all day
In front of the television
They paint their fingers and toes

And keep them like hedges
Around the compound
African women must be different

They need to work and produce
Many sons for the tribe
My wife lived in the West for

Too long and has forgotten
Our sacred rights and customs
She is unable to cook our foods

She depends on fast foods
To feed the children
And they are unfit for work in the fields

White women are lazy
Sometimes even crazy
They have no more than two children

Because they haven't any farms
My life is ruined and I fear
The worst for the upbringing of

Our children. Their hands will be
Soft and their language strange
To the ears of the village elders

One day I hope my wife **will** come
To her senses and take her
Responsibility seriously as mother

# Home is Darkness

I crawled about in the darkness
of my room. No streetlights cast
Their sinewy shadows about

The air was heavy with thoughts
Of putrid bodies, meat to maggots
I shuddered as layers of pain

Peeled from my body and like rain
Dropped and widened into circles
My blood congealed into icicles

And I longed to go home
My adulthood unfolded
A lack of knowledge about Africa

Corrupted colonial teachings formed
An unyielding character of right
And wrong, and the books I read

Revealed that Africa was dark
That night I beheld the blackness
And was caught up in its fear

Then I remembered that I was there
In rural East Africa amid the mysterious
throng. Passing time revealed that

I lived a lie all those years
My ancestors still lived in me
And I was home once again

# Dawn of a New Year

Daylight came oh so early
On this landlocked border
Where sunshine showed its splendour

In azure and splashing white
Grey converged on the skyline
And red cries came from Kampala's hills

I looked to the encircling peaks
painted in rainbow colours
where jubilation bullets rang out

The music blared across busy roads
And untamed shouts ascended skywards
There was a new dawn, a new birth

There were new dreams for new things
And chimes told time of the passing
Of an old year, lost in the mists

Yet the sun still shone in its usual place
And shone its light with intensity
Night killed the emerging spirit

# Drums of War

Today the lake is quiet
The ancestral spirits
Have calmed its waters

Lake Victoria points the way home
But the children are afraid to return
Drums of war beat the death rhythm

At the water's edge, mothers call
For children snatched away
To be soldiers for liberation

The generals think their cause is right
And so pillage the villages in sight
The young revolutionaries are smitten

The dogs of war are let loose,
ravaging all. There is no surrender
When tribal honour is at stake

Come, come, come to the lake
This pearl we shall retake
Come and comfort your mother's heart

# Pearl of Africa

I have no sea, yet I am a pearl
Lakes wrap their lips and swirl
Brackish water down my middle

I am a pearl because people love me
Strip my veins and find cobalt and copper
Oil will soon twist my nappy hair into curls

My beauty lies in my resplendent skin
Strength comes from ugali and matoke
My poverty shines in enamel bowls

Of cassava, yam and African sweet potatoes
Examine the blends of my natural colours
Richly textured with black and indigo blue

I do not eat rich foods like steak and fish
Rice and soybeans are not on the menu
But I dine simply with a pot of lentil stew

Give me chipati and flatbread
And a side dish of groundnuts sauce
Poor man food keeps me afloat and healthy

# With Age Comes Respect

I love Uganda, pearl of Africa
In the streets honey rains from many tongues
And keep me alert to new possibilities

I hear Luganda greetings and Busoga goodbyes
Spiced with English, "you're welcome"
Jambo my long lost relatives. I hear you

The white of my hair bathed in
Dazzling sunlight, reflects the core
of my African heritage. Here I am*!*

I am mzee, an old man
Respected, reverenced and uplifted
Knowledge is the shade on my head

The young flock to me searching for wisdom
Like the Makerere storks strutting across
The silent lawns on the university grounds

I am showered with deference
There is no room to falter
Here I am a quiet grandfather

## Farewell Uganda

I came, I saw and am yet
to conquer your ring of mountains
I saw pregnant hills about to deliver
scar-tissue of crags, child birth
of houses sprawling legs of bastardy

I heard the groans of disturbed valleys,
overworked by trudging cattle,
men in battle gear fighting for Japanese
imports of diesel constipation in old
cars, trucks and other vainglorious vehicles

I enjoyed the fruits of your womb
Mounds of matooke, pineapple, papaya
green-skinned melon, red pressed
inside, banana bruised dry and sweet
lust of stomach rumbling digestion

The stork woke me in the morning
and claimed my reverie with
child calls of hah! hah! hah!
I blamed the child next door
for its hurt noises of poor quality

Farewell to your prison of smoke
where bricks toke until browned
drunk and cured for building
the next generation of Western castles
in the skin of this pearly nation

Goodbye world of boda boda jostling
for scraps of people to earn a living;
to right and left handed motorists

who fail to see the tongues of tourists
begging for directions in this Kampala maze

Farewell to arms of gun toting
brothers who secure the people by
standing at the corners of thieving
rogues, protecting the wind and sun
I will miss your uninformed dress

Au revoir room locks and jingling
keys, of train wreck gates keeping
out polished thieves in the act of
revenge against the modern rich
I'll see you soon enough

*A la prochaine mon amour Uganda*
bodies thin while protruding butts
of women insure a good crop of children
I return to my arctic freeze
where the cold breeze keeps me warm

# Jamaican Voices
# from the Forest

# March Pen

Thunder clap of words
Ricochetes off zinc flesh
And hug streets scarred by pot holes

Children rouse laughter
At this tenement's border
While heat waves bathe the day

Ribs of houses buckle from rot
Too many children languish from pot
Yet this place is called home

Home the seat of the heart
Beats and courses poverty vines
Through veins of neglect and longing

I long for cooling wata
To soothe brittle sinews
And closure that brings peace

No peace comes from the quiet of sleep
No cockcrows can wake a body
That is drugged by fire-breathing sun

# No Release

You call me brother in this cement slammer
This steel's too thick to bind us together
I'm doing six years for a crime
The President of the United States enshrined

Cousin Bill took his spliff all the way to the Hill
And conducted his foreign affairs with aplomb still
Here my joints creek like the steel in this cell
While you join with the force to wish me well

True, I had problems with the stuff; starved
While the biblical farmers reaped the harvest
They drove Ferraris at the back of the house
And asked my mother when I'll be free

Here, there is no release for the black man
No one-sixth or two-thirds images appear
The maximum time is de full t'ing, Sar
There is no kindness; all is fair in this war

I and I find it hard fi communicate wi the man
Muh island rhythms wid a chupse of frustration
And im seh mi lost control in this great confusion
Parole Board nuh lissen to we plea for leniency

They seh dat de police seh dat all Jah's chillun dem
Belong to some nefarious gang, some J'can possee
Rastafari believe that Jah in im glory mek we
Fi understan' dat dey is two kind o'mercy

There's freedom with forgiveness and there's
Freedom with mental chains gridlocking we brains
But mi seh fi unlock the gates of these prisons
Since justice is the basis of Canadian democracy

## Ownway Piccanni

"Bwoy stop de pounding o'dem drum in mi 'ead,"
Granny said, as I curled mi budding dread.

"When I was young, I had was to walk country road
Searching fi a job and guilt was mi load.

Nine piccanni home wid gran' muhmah
Mi eldest daughter was practising negromancy,

Trying hard fi ketch Massa Barry's youngest bwoy
"I still remember the smell o' de herbs – lavender

And Rose oil and de full strength o' bay leaf -- and
mi child stepping so, she eyes straight on de prize,

And you here now, a generation, with no tradition,
brekking down ear drum with riddums of freedom.

I say practise negromancy and turn the world topsy-turvy.
Practise negromancy and find a new reality.

The roof pees like an old man
        With stricture
    Wata flows, drip
      Plop, plop
      Plop

The bucket fills and splatters
      Breaking up required sleep
        Eyelids
        Flicker
        Flicker
        Stop

The poet takes a peep
      And watches the wata
        Swirling
        Swirling
        Churning noises

Voices are silent in these drips
      Of running time
        Flip
        Flip
        Flip the bucket

Repeat the process while ahead
      Let's see the results
        In the bed
        In the bed
        Waiting

# Tenement

I am a prisoner here
I am bound without chains
In a house with iron bars

My space is restricted by zinc walls
producing sharp gashes of tetanus
I dare not try to escape

My nights are filled with sweet melodies
Boom ba boom ba boing boing
The boom box contains me

I fight the stench of my bath
And box with those who dare
Pierce my skin with buzzing needles

I am well fed with mealy pap
And mango juice that zap
My arteries curdling Noni sweetness

I look for rescue in the tunnels
Of my thoughts, but fear blocks
My path for I am with family

## City Dwellers

This city
      Is the home
            Of poverty

Rings of smoke
      Pungently inflate
            Snow-lined lungs

Feet stride up the narrow lanes
      Defeat lurks behind bushes
            Revenge is held high

Death lies in her fulsome bosom
      She drinks the juices of lust
            And uses banana leaves as cover

Early morning creates new designs
      While noonday executes plans
            Of cunning

Children walk half-naked
      In alleys of dread
            Curls tight 'pon dem head

The city seat of government
      Bloats itself with the bodies
            Of fat cats, pigs and gangsters

# Our Future

Amidst the din of noise
The children poise themselves
For repeats of yesterday's lies

Their mooma seh
A bright tomorrow go come
This is the text message of the day

Then swarms of gal pickney descend
'pon corner roads dem exposed
Bottoms inviting larceny *dem*

The boys hold up their crotches wid sell phone
Rings and chatter, flashing Lasco teeth, white smile
Poopa stay home while Mooma walks a mile

Fi feed pickney breeding lives
In pregnant succession
We build di nation 'pon dese.

# Reggae Breeze

The blood boils and bubbles within
This cauldron of a tropic body

Blood vessels bring forth heat,
Spew rage of sweat spumes

Into stricken streets where cries are silent
Today there is peace in the Pen

Silence bows down and waits
For a shower of rain to pass by

A lizard crawls in camouflage green
Inna suitcase from a foreign

Licks his lips and cools himself
In the shade of a man's brief

He shares a moment and moves on
A fan blows reggae breeze

# Linstead Market

This is the legacy of my people
From Africa to the Caribee isles

They drift along the streets with trinkets
Trying to eke food from rough garments

Buy a likkle som'ting mi got fi feed pickney
At home whither shall they roam

Through moving traffic they attempt a sale
From Kampala to Nairobi from

Bridgetown to Kingston, every body
Come selling, but nabady go buy

# Darkness

Darkness is Lethe's bastard child
She is conceived in hillside caves

And is whelped in Jamaica's wild
Of music; of people massing

With protesting placards
Against the injustice of incarceration

Darkness seizes day thoughts
And transforms them into murderous

Stabs of machete chops and bullets
ignite midnight revelry in the pens

Love conceives in wanton daylight
And reflects horrors in mind caves

Greed impairs poverty's vision
And goodness escapes in kadooment

## Light of Day

Light of day is pressure cooled with anger
And gay intentions are ruled by fear

The hush of things here
Pulsate into swirls of rivalry

At the setting sun a woman sweeps
Up her young son and they run

An AK 47 hangs from his hand.
He is going to be a policeman

He is justicier of freedom and peace
Him lets bullets fly inna yard

Bringing the just and unjust
To an irrevocable judgment,

Reserved only for the Almighty
Judge not lest you be judged

In the police shoot out the high command
Seh we mustn't judge di motive

Of di police dem fi protecting demselves
From unrighteous slaughter

There is a shoot out wi nine victims
The police escape injury

Oh death, where is your sting?
Life is expendable in a living being

## Coppa Sold Here

There's a new practice
In beautiful Jamaica;
Men hunting graves fi coppa

Wi sledge hamma dem
Bruck di cement tombs
Disenfranchising di dead

Wa gwaan here in wi country
When di dead dread peace
Dis grave robbin must cease

Wi ninety per cent o' people
Lackin food and proper edication
It's bound to be ruction

Gangs have no civility or respect for hurt
In dis Jamaican society
And di big men dem beggin

Jamaicans a foreign fi come home
Fi prop up de country wi blood money
To stop di brain drain

# The Call

Inna di alley way
     Way of ownway pickney
A gal chile stand like a
     Cotton tree, fluffy, fluffy
Goat eyes heng 'pon hips
     Lips of want speak
Nine mouths to feed
     Nine bodies in need of heat
And there is another belly protrusion

Lips suck from bitter, lumpy breasts
Hands crawl around spindly legs
While the numbers grow
     One, two, three skip
To the loo my darling;
     Six, seven, this is
The gateway to heaven
     In stereophonic cries
The air is filled with wants:
Wants of food

Wants of clothes
     Wants of shelter
We a go betta Jamaica

## II

Come home from a foreign my bretheren
We must lessen di brain drain
Taste di sweet, sweet orange juice
     There are pleasures still in dark places;
Pleasures inna di park of heroes

Pleasures call fi an absent poopa
On di canal banks
Shaking down di shopkeepas
For today's debt fi child support
Gone missing inna di rainforest

The dogs of night whelp while the bulls
Maraude village strangers,
Rangers in di dark
Di howls wake Miss Mardi
From she grave yard sleep
In di deep, in di deep
By and by, we shall meet
On dat beautiful sure

## III

Di gal is no more than
Seventeen
Seventeen an' she preen
She self with a beak
Of wandering lip gloss
She lips like mango in season
The reason fi dis life
Is encased in Adam's tomb
First curse of disobedience

She offers repentance again
For millennial curses that
Heng on black males who carry assault weapons
They behead udders in the deep of night
When clouds sleep
And di moon try fi peep past demons

Trampling truth
Revelation's horsemen of war/victory
Death and defiance
Salvation to come


**IV**

Him read di psalms 'pon time's sands
A cooling breath of wata
Rushes headlong through the villages
Despair crushing March Pen
Duncan Pen's neighbor
Down river there is a sweet refrain
In di sweet by and by we shall meet fi sure
'Cause death is di wages fi sin
And poverty and hunger rain bullets
On sons and daughters

Look at God's pe'ple dem
Nah go to di taba... echo
Tabernacle of worship wid bullets
Pluggin' holes wey dem lan'
Satan tryin' fi out do di Saviour
Wi false promise of manna
Rainin' dung fires from heaven
Ravishin' di sanctuary

Mi seh fi worship God honly
Fi dere's no otha
Bow down in oly penitence
Han' ask fi liberation

## V

Di politicians dem
      Pour libations along di steps
To glory; brimstone an' fire following
      And dem followers wi orange hope
Wave Jamaican flags inna
Di face o' starvation
Di opposition promise mo' bettah
      Days fi come 'cause we Jamaicans
Know how fi celelebrate plenty hurt
      Hollering
      Bawling
Bowing down, low down
      To di groun' of desolation
Daughtas of Babylon

We raise wi weed
      Speed of high
Speed of speech to serve Jah
      Unknown god of Africa
Hell fire emerge inna di church yard
      And worshippers wi card-
Carrying faith offa dem deeds
      Fi cleansing blood
Look to di hills fi salvation

## VI

There'll be peace in di lan' one day
      Bolt wi gold hole di future
Run fast home at last
   maica land of beauty
     t of many one nation a plenty
      Many tribes but no salvation

Come home mi brothers
> Follow dem mi sisters

Mooma call, poopa have child support at last

Leh we a go build castles in di san
> Dat rest on seashore

Leh we ago build we future
> Dis is Jamaica we highlan' inna di sun

In di light o' we god
> From Africa till now

Sweet taste of liberty
> From raiding villages of Ashanti

# Lookin' Hup!

My eyes look to the Blue Mountains
Covered with this African hue

I sing of the beauty up there
In layers of dire poverty

The mists of the valley hide
Runnels of vibrant water

Drowning out the rock fest
The downspout of rain

In valley gullies below
Where corrugated peaks rise

Amidst the blueness of thoughts
There is a beauty in Jamaica

Where mountains collide in
Newness of grandeur

Clouds clash in mutinous thunder
And intransigent lightning

Calls forth fire in the night sky
Where the gods dwell in splendor

Down below in the valley of stress
And mountain debris the best

Of the poor sell borrowed fruits
To grow breast feeding girls

Wearing flesh suits of fat
Here the rata-tat- tat

Of gummed lives upon naked hills
Bring no mercy from the scorching hills

I stop to view the monuments
Of love that created one people

Out of many flings lies in the eyes
The more him climb, the more di monkey

him expose that law and order
Flows down to the revisiting
Beauty that is my Jamaica

# They Came to Seize

Twisting cords of web mass
     The spider's last

Resort at entrapment
     Death is robed in grass

Within ravines and gullies
narrowing life between mountain slides

The castle on the other side triumphs amid leaves
Remaining green for a season

Fear fogs up all lens of human and cameras
     As steps put-put with constipation

A prayer is uttered in silence
     For the rocks may come

Down, descend to worship
     At the foothills of desolation

The shepherd gazes at goats
     Grazing the hills bare

Wild dogs howl in the night air
     As death curls up at roadside

Ribs of desperation cancel hunger pains
     While unguarded mouths chew empty words

Buzzards buzz the roads
     To dislodge blood stains

In graveyards of potholes
      This is my land of woods

And rivers floating pickney down
To the churning sea of want

## Joy Inna Mornin'

Mi sing because mi a happy
Mi sing because mi a free

Di Koreans own we electricity
And di Chinese take we money

Fi roads dat link we country
The European Union rapes us

An' gives our police shelter from di rain
We are beggars free, depending

On American larceny while Canada
Sustains us with in and out RBC

Our reggae brand is free
All over di world and culture

Piracy is our royalty provider
We a dance, we a sing

All dat is Jamaica is in ganja
We shall not want in dis lan' o'plenty

# Noise

Noise is calling hard-ear pickney
Noise is barking dogs fighting

Di darkness outside di door
Noise is children chupsing loud

At empty calls from lazy parents
For a bokkle o' wata next to dem

Inna di refrigerator nearby
Noise is honking horns vexing

Morning quiet of choking smoke
Noise is parents boxing children down

Noise is Ma—yet—te! Mayette!
Bri—an—na! Brianna

Shakira! Squeals of electric calls
Inna day or inna night

Noise is TV masquerading till morning
Noise is di antidote fi unfulfilled needs

With pleasures of hearing
An' not responding

Noise is badly crafted reggae songs
Eva body wanting to be Bob Marley

Noise is di precursor a di revolution
We need fi a change dis nation

Noise is political insurrection
In dis here Babyland

# Across the Hills from Mandeville

Sheets of rain came to the mountain again
Cutting the air in thin slices on the range

I saw the decapitation of tree tops
And heard the tears from cloud drops

The air is refreshingly pure up here
Putrid smells and city dwellers disappear

In the cool of the evening all is clear
The terraced hills peer over lazy valleys

Retirees take evening naps in the shadows
Of drooping trees and foreign dwellings

If mountains could talk, they would declare
That all works well in mountain air

# Reunited

(For Orlando and Joyce)

Fifty years of broken sights
Morphe into greetings of delight

The greetings lead to dining, talking
The past crashing into the present

Dagnation's heavy stamp lies on
Aging faces weeping willows of one tree

And so two cousins merge again
With stories that came with the rain

# Mountain Breeze

A mellow breeze stretches across the mountain
The air languishes in the evening shadow

Gone is the damning smoke of city dumps
Gone is gasping lungs for freshets of blood

The clouds feed on verdant leaves
Leaving traces of blue upon their hues

Oh for a life upon the hills
Where the gods sip fresh dewdrops

# The Valley

*(In memory of Aunt Ida March 20, 1918*
*– September 5, 2011)*

Ida sits in the valley
     Vision is silenced
But there is a voice
     Whispering
         Mocking
            Present reality

There is solemnity in the air
     Mocking of whispers
Sadness rides the eyes
     Pelting
         Thoughts
            Slow to regenerate

At ninety three birthdays sput
     Into sudden action
I was born March 20,1918
     Arousing
         Recollections
         Of death-struct daughters

Final moments push to the fore
     My son is in America
She racks her brain silently
     Unwinding **skeins** of thoughts
         Teasing
            The memory of a poem

She recites two lines
Trying to unravel knots of time
The mouth mutters the verse

Eyes look up nothing
Feeling
Backtracking
Under trod time

"Some people go to church to talk
Some people go to church to meet friends
But I go to church
To praise the Lord"
Then there's a drawl
Memory flies away

She listens to unseen voices
As feeble feet dangle
Limply from her bed
Time erasing
A body fading in floral green sheets
Strength forces last goodbyes

Parting words from niece and aunt
Ring sad melodies from the heart
Parting from the valley where no hope
Lies in surrounding hills
Understanding slips
Nothing is left to celebrate

## Three Old Men

Three old men sit
In three thatched huts
Their dreads flopping about their ears
They agree that they came from Africa as Ashanti
Warring against the British in Trewlaney with machetes

Chopping a path to liberation aided by Nanny the maroon
Their scarred teeth of brown
Reveal their place
In the struggle for liberation

Jah's children
Are errant Rastafarian
 held up high
Inna di rainforest
 calling for a holy war of salvation

## Fading Light

I sit here
>>In the lonely
>>>>Light

The sun is there
>>Bedding down finally
>>>>In the soft night

Thoughts roam
>>Here and everywhere
>>>>As I brood about life

The wife left
>>Amidst intense daylight
>>>>Under brisk heat

Now the crickets call
>>And my fears crawl
>>>>To a pregnant surface

I am here alone
>>The trees protect me
And console me at twilight

# Unity

The Caribbean Sea
     Is a trickster
         Beckoning
         Hauling
         Calling
         Dragging under

The Caribbean Sea
Says Jamaica is nice
     A cunning marauder
         Enrapturing
         Murdering beauty
         Stealing foreign vices

Di gals dem pretty
     Surrounded by pickney
         Lips of mango juice
         Dripping
         For Wray and Nephew
         Standin' inna di wrong pew

# Song Bird

The wretched of the earth
Walk this blessed land

The poor keep company
With the venerable Bob Marley

He is the song bird of liberation
In this here Babyland

Freedom is Morgan tipsy in his hammock
Freedom is Mooma callin her likkle bwoy

Fi come carry him Poopa drink
Of Cocoa tea inna tin cup

People sing redemption songs
Help is wanted to grow di economy

Under di banner o' liberty
Di people dem bruck ya wi misery

# Heroes Park

Mi soon come back yuh hear
Heroes echo the sweet refrain

With a cloud wrap they hover
Over di lan' again, no shame

Heroes in their marble homes
Sing of one love, a no name brand

Peace rains no more over this broken land
Where leaders offer the promise of salvation

Oh Jamaica yo cause mi yeye
To wata every time I see you

Shrouded in regal splendor
The rich live high on the hog

The poor eat, drink and are merry
In their fatness, in their hurting

In their want of newness, a desire
For the right to be free

# Serenade

When I look into your eyes
I see time's passing melodies

You are beautiful Jamaica
You wear colours of pride

You are real nice cavorting
With those who offer no spice

You are in bed with China, Europe
America and South Korea

They suck your breasts dry
Leaving behind, bastard children to cry

Your highways stretch to China
And your wantonness calls for tolls

France puts her hand in your bosom
And sets up her port of call

South Korea lights up your night
And the weed reduces your will to fight

# Summer Fest

Come home to Jamaica
Where the summer breeze refreshes

Out of many are your people of Black,
Of Brown of White, without tact

I hear your croaking voice Jamaica
Dripping dizzying songs in the sudden rain

Your poor of black soil are downtrodden
Seeking Marley's emancipation

I long for a Jamaica free
Of foreign debt and IMF calamity

Then our songs of freedom will resonate
In every nook and cranny in the state

# Fruits of Life

The ackee tree
      Forges her way upward

Twisting her body
      Around a Noni tree

Together they kiss and support
      Each other in the throes of passion

The Noni leaves cool
      The achee's brood

Both produce poor man's food
      Anti-oxidants and yellow meat

Collide and drop sustaining life at their feet
      Come eat the fruits of hunger freedom